No Place like Home

F-Pentatonic Series Book 2

Jai Schelbach   Andrés González

Copyright © 2021 Jai Schelbach
No place like Home Self-published
jaischelbach@gmail.com
www.jaischelbach.com
All rights reserved.
No part of this publication may be reproduced, stored in a retrieval system, stored in a database and / or published in any form or by any means, electronic, mechanical, photocopying, recording or otherwise, without the prior written permission of the publisher.
ISBN: 978-0-6488904-3-0
Softcover edition

Dedicated to:

My wife, Sarah.
You make our house a home and fill my heart with love.
Forever yours - J.S. xoxo

On the Jackson's farm
down Wildflower Lane,
lived a turtle called Tom,
whose life was mundane.
Until one day
not long ago,
he learned two notes
one high and one low.
Ever since then
he sings 'See Saw',
all the day long
from dusk till dawn.

Then one fine day
he planned to go out,
to Piccolo Pond
where water lilies sprout.
He arrived at the pond
it was filled to the brim,
he gazed at the flowers
and went for a swim.
Then...

Tom heard a commotion
up near the old house,
a black and white cat
was chasing a mouse.
They dashed through the garden
in a blur of light,
they sped past the deck
and slipped out of sight.
One moment later
the chase reappeared
mouse rushed to the pond
the cat right on his rear.
Then with a dive
Mouse plunged down his hole,
Cat gave one last pounce
but did miss his goal.

Tom was soooooo close
he froze with fear,
but the cat was distracted
by his itchy left ear.

He scratched and he scraped,
he twisted and turned,
a tangle of legs
that wriggled and squirmed
When...

All of a sudden
a tiny wee speck
flew off the cats ear
and crashed in a wreck!
Landing hard on the ground
it trembled in shock,

then ducked for cover
behind a large rock.
After easing his itch
the cat skulked away,
He'd catch that mouse
another fine day.

Relaxing a little
(as the cat had moved on),
Tom went to find out
where that speck had gone.
Behind the large rock
was a pile of trash,
including some paper
where he'd seen the speck dash.
Tom spoke to the pile,
"Is anybody there?"
But the speck remained hidden
'cause he'd had such a scare.
Tom rummaged through the pile
checking inside an old sock,
Then peaked under some paper
beside the big rock.
"Don't hurt me, don't hurt me!
Please let me be!
My name is Florence,"
pleaded the flea.

Don't worry, Florence
please do not weep,
but do tell me how
you arrived in this heap?"

Realizing Tom
would not hurt a rose,
she told him her story…
this is how it goes.

"I've lived my whole life
on the black and white cat
Mr. Bing is his name
and he IS rather fat.
But the last few days
he's been out at night,
he got locked outside
and could NOT get a bite.

Hungry as ever
he prowled 'round the house,
when approaching the chimney
he discovered the mouse.
A frantic chase started
I held on so tight,
I gripped his left ear
with all of my might.
So hard was my grip
it gave him an itch,
that's when his back leg
started to twitch.
And now I am here
very alone,
no food, no friends
no family, no home..."

Whilst Florence kept talking
Tom's eyes were drawn,
to the paper by the rock
that was looking forlorn.
Was that half a symbol?
Were those dots and lines?
He interrupted Florence,
"It's music, what a find!"

Florence turned around
perplexed and surprised.
What were these strange marks
in front of her eyes?

"I've found a new song!
It's called 'Snail Snail',
let me read you these notes
I hope I don't fail."
Tom sang out loud
and right near the end,
he discovered a new note
he'd never seen penned.
It sat on line four
near the notes that he knew,
Above C on space three
and A on space two.

Pondering the problem
Tom had an idea,
then said in a flurry,
"Let's get out of here!
We'll solve all our troubles
both yours and mine,
with my special friend
who's simply divine."

Tom led the way
the path mostly straight,
and soon they arrived
at Treble Clef gate.
Luce welcomed Tom back
"Oh, what a fine day!
Now, tell me what brings you
along this way?"
"I've found a new song
it's called 'Snail Snail'!
But firstly meet Florence
I must tell you her tale.

So Tom told Luce
that Florence had no home.
and about her misfortunes
that now she's alone.
Luce replied "See that door
at space number one?
Settle in, meet some friends,
then go have some fun."
So Florence snuggled in
to the posts first floor,
it was cosy and warm
she could NOT ask for more.

Now...
"Tell me about the song,"
Luce said to Tom.
"You mentioned 'Snail Snail',
but explain what is wrong?"

"C and A are ok
I know them from 'See Saw',
but I cannot make sense
of the note on line four."

"Aha!" Luce exclaimed
and she gave a small grin,
"The note on line four
belongs to Dylan."
"You mean the dragonfly?"
Tom slowly asked.
"The one who wears
a cap and a mask?"
"Exactly," replied Luce
"Let me call him for you."
With a zip and zoom
out Dylan flew.
"How are you Tom?"
he announced with glee.
"I'm well, I've just found
a new note to read."
"I wonder if Aria,
Cadence and you,
could help me sing
my new 'Snail' tune?

Aria jumped out
and giggled, "For sure!"
Cadence grumped about;
Dylan zipped to line four!
So Tom sang the song
with the new letter D,
Entertaining his friends
including the flea.

He thanked Luce again
he bid them farewell,
and tucked his new song
into his shell.
He set off for home
singing the tune,
all the way back
to Kent's Lagoon.

SNAIL SNAIL

Snail, snail, snail, snail, go a-round and round and round.

ABOUT

"Music is a more potent instrument than any other for education because rhythm and harmony find their way into the inward places of the soul."

Plato

Music education is and always has been in a state of constant change, even since the days of Plato. In the 21st Century, the difference has been magnified by the speed of technology and continuous connection to the world around us. However, this means that we can sometimes forget the original purposes of teaching methods such as Kodály, Orff, or Dalcroze, which were tools to help achieve the unified goal of making music. My hope in writing this series of books is that they would bridge the gap from solfège to reading letter names through the guise of storytelling.

To aid children's recollection of the story and support the learning outcomes, I have also included some free resources such as an mp3 of the song 'Snail Snail.' These resources can be found at www.jaischelbach.com.

It doesn't matter how you use this book or how old you are. As long as the story reaches into your heart and moves you, then this is the first step to understanding the power of a story and the heartbeat of music.

May you always keep singing, learning, and growing so that the beauty of music continues to pass from one generation to the next!

JAI SCHELBACH

Jai grew up in the Scenic Rim area of South East Queensland and has many fond memories of living in Kalbar and Boonah. In 2005, he finished his Bachelor Music/Bachelor Education degree at UNSW. He currently lives on the sunny Gold Coast and teaches music to students from Kindergarten through to Grade 5.

ANDRÉS GONZÁLEZ

Andrés was born on the east side of Colombia. After obtaining his Bachelor Degree in Graphic Design, he decided to specialize in telling stories through illustration. Today he lives in Amsterdam and enjoys creating storybooks for children.

www.ingramcontent.com/pod-product-compliance
Lightning Source LLC
Chambersburg PA
CBHW050854010526
44107CB00048BA/1607